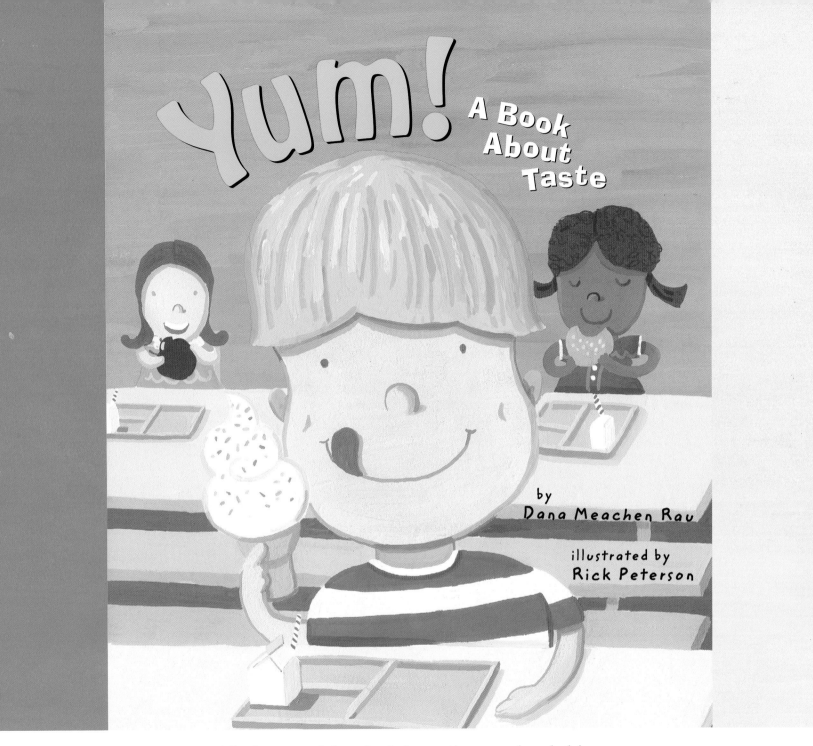

Yum! A Book About Taste

by
Dana Meachen Rau

illustrated by
Rick Peterson

Thanks to our advisers for their expertise, research, and advice:

Angela Busch, M.D., All About Children Pediatrics, Minneapolis, Minnesota

Susan Kesselring, M.A., Literacy Educator
Rosemount-Apple Valley-Eagan (Minnesota) School District

PICTURE WINDOW BOOKS
Minneapolis, Minnesota

Managing Editor: Catherine Neitge
Creative Director: Terri Foley
Art Director: Keith Griffin
Editor: Christianne Jones
Designer: Nathan Gassman
Page Production: Picture Window Books
The illustrations in this book are gouache paintings.

Picture Window Books
5115 Excelsior Boulevard
Suite 232
Minneapolis, MN 55416
877-845-8392
www.picturewindowbooks.com

Printed in the United States of America.

Library of Congress Cataloging-in-Publication Data
Rau, Dana Meachen, 1971-
Yum! : a book about taste / by Dana Meachen Rau ;
illustrated by Rick Peterson.
p. cm. — (Amazing body)
Includes bibliographical references and index.
ISBN 1-4048-1021-8 (hardcover)
1. Taste—Juvenile literature. I. Peterson, Rick.
II. Title. III. Series.

QP456.R38 2005
612.8'7—dc22   2004019173

Rumble, grumble, growl!

Your stomach is telling you that it's time for lunch.

You can't wait to dig in and taste your food!

Taste is one of your five senses.

Your tongue is the only muscle you can see on the outside of your body.

Your tongue is the muscle in charge of tasting. It can also sense if food or drink is hot or cold.

5

Your tongue helps you talk and taste what you eat and drink.

La La La La La La La La La Lunch!

Taste tells your body if something is good to eat.

Your sense of taste also warns your body when something is rotten. Rotten food could make your body sick.

Your tongue is covered with tiny bumps and spikes. They are called papillae.

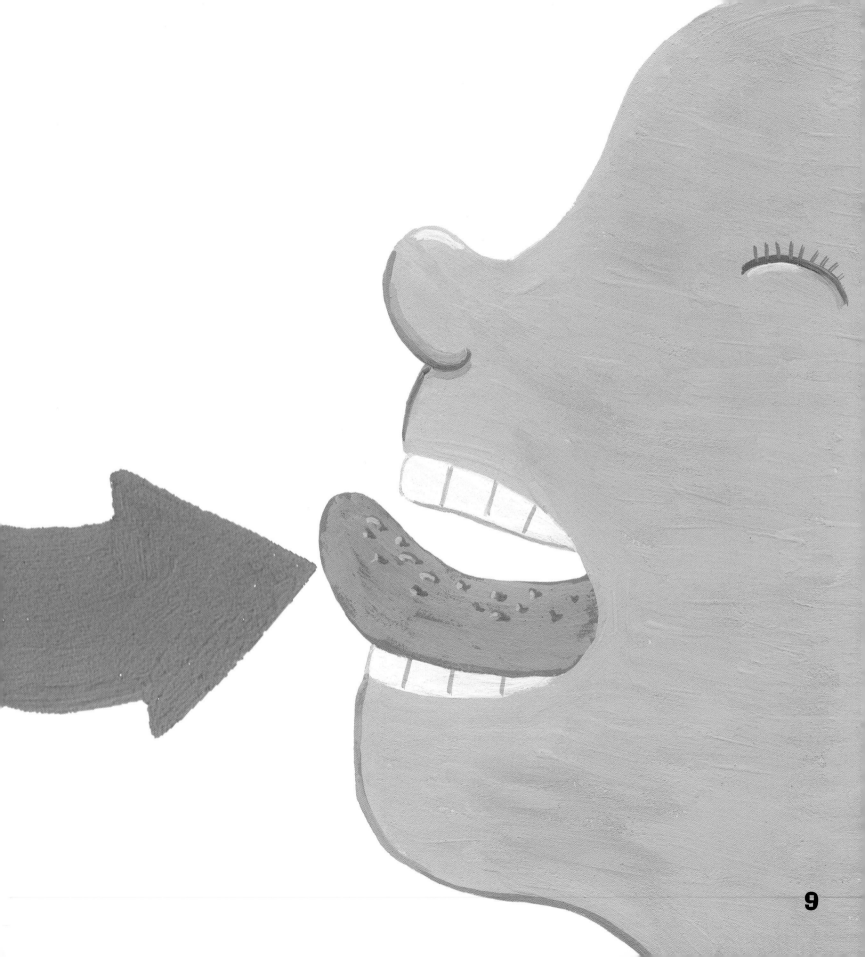

The papillae grab onto the food in your mouth.

They help your
tongue move
the food
around
inside your
mouth as
you chew.

As you chew the food, it mixes with a liquid in your mouth called saliva. Saliva makes the food soft and juicy.

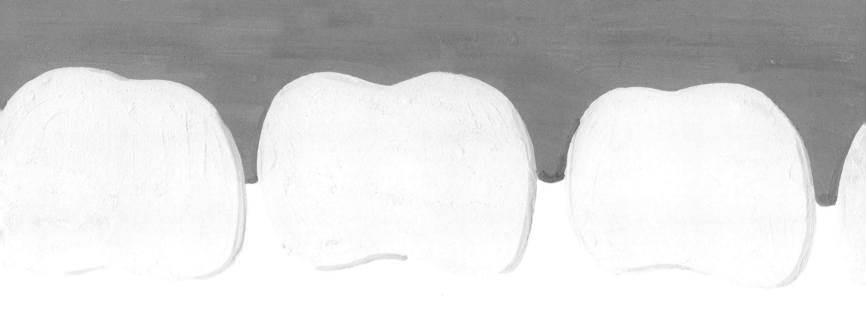

The juices carry the flavor from the food. These juices get caught in the papillae and seep down into your taste buds.

Most flavors are sweet, salty, sour, or bitter. Different parts of your tongue are more sensitive to these certain tastes. You taste sweet on the tip of your tongue, salty on the tip and sides, sour on the sides, and bitter on the back.

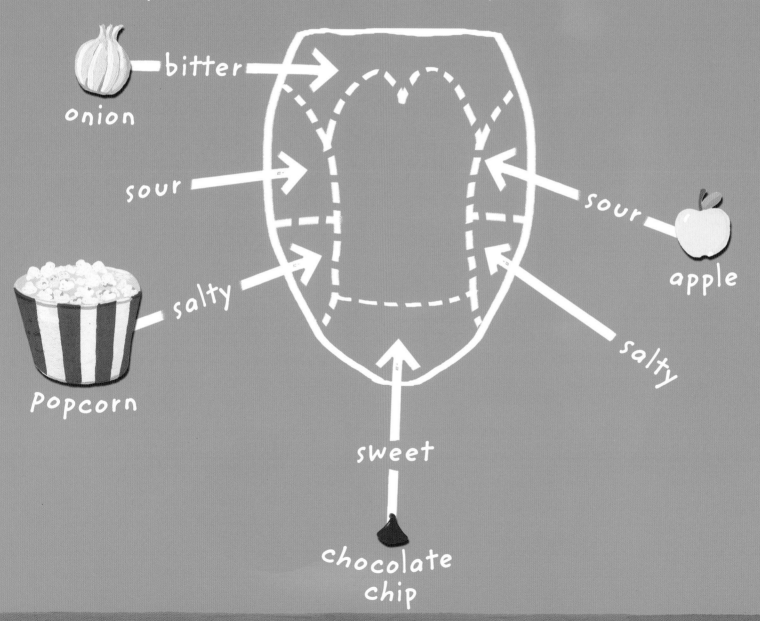

onion — bitter

sour

Popcorn — salty

sour — apple

salty

sweet

chocolate chip

Taste buds
are found all over
your tongue. They
are also on the roof
and sides of your
mouth and in
your throat.

Your taste buds help you taste food.
They are even smaller than papillae.
Taste buds are made up of tiny
cells grouped together like an onion.

Your taste buds are replaced every week.

Your taste buds are connected to your nerves. Your nerves are connected to your brain.

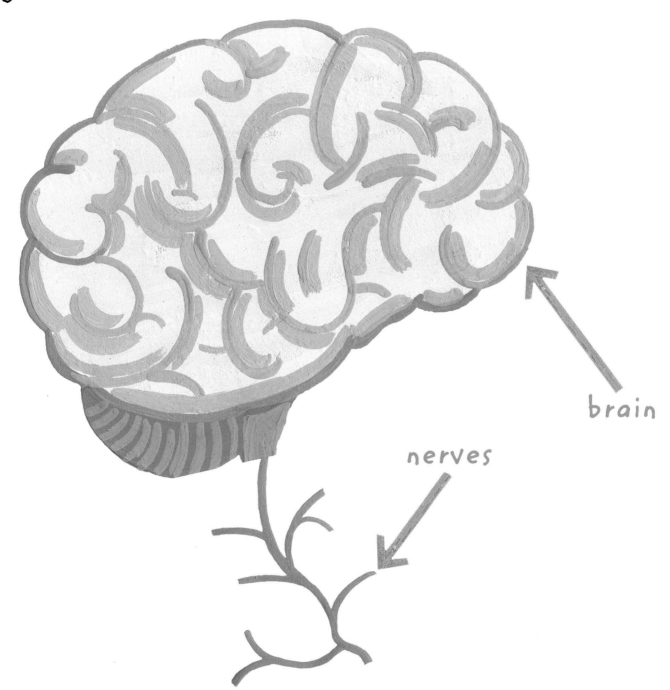

brain

nerves

When a flavor reaches a taste bud, the taste bud sends a message along your nerves to your brain. Your brain tells you what food you are tasting.

Your brain can remember tastes you have had before. Your brain will also know if you are trying a new food.

19

Everyone likes different foods because everyone's body is a little different.

Even though people like different things, everyone has great taste!

Taste Diagram

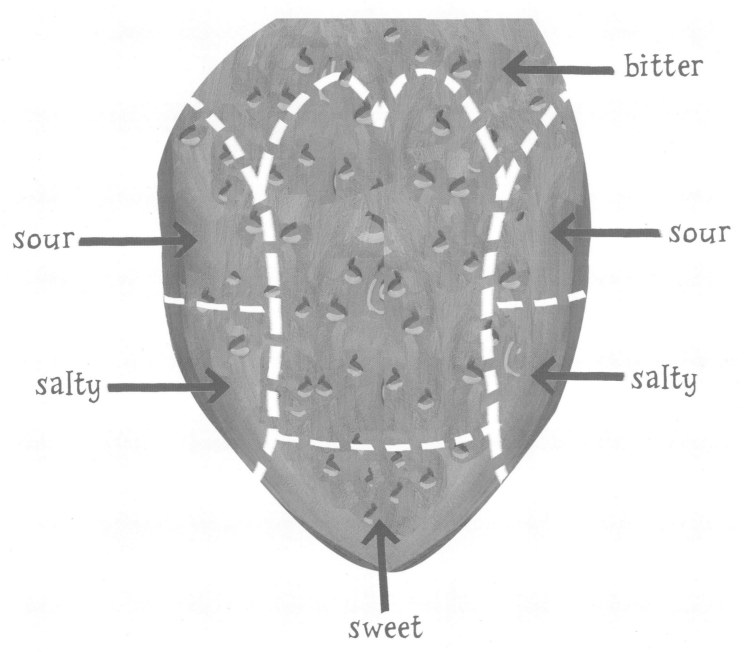

Fun Facts

- Your tongue can move in many ways. Some people can curl their tongue, and some people can flip their tongue.

- When you are very hungry, your mouth makes extra saliva. You might even say, "My mouth is watering!"

- Your sense of smell and sense of taste are closely related. When you have a cold and your nose is stuffy, it is often hard to taste what you eat and drink.

- You have almost 10,000 taste buds in your mouth. In general, girls have more taste buds than boys.

Glossary

muscles—the parts of your body in charge of movement

nerves—cords running through your body that get and give messages to your brain

papillae—tiny bumps and spikes that cover your tongue

saliva—a liquid in your mouth that helps make food soft

taste buds—small bundles of cells that taste food

To Learn More

At the Library

Cobb, Vicki. *Your Tongue Can Tell: Discover Your Sense of Taste.* Brookfield, Conn.: Millbrook Press, 2000.

Cole, Joanna. *You Can't Smell a Flower with Your Ear! All About Your Five Senses.* New York: Grosset and Dunlap, 1994.

Fowler, Allan. *Let's Talk About Tongues.* New York: Children's Press, 1997.

On the Web

FactHound offers a safe, fun way to find
Web sites related to this book. All of the sites
on FactHound have been researched by our staff.

1. Go to www.facthound.com

2. Type in this special code: 1404810218

3. Click on the fetch it button.

Your trusty FactHound will fetch the best sites for you!

Look for all of the books in the Amazing Body series:

Bend and Stretch: Learning About Your Bones and Muscles

Breathe In, Breathe Out: Learning About Your Lungs

Gurgles and Growls: Learning About Your Stomach

Look! A Book About Sight

Look, Listen, Taste, Touch, and Smell: Learning About Your Five Senses

Shhhh… A Book About Hearing

Sniff, Sniff: A Book About Smell

Soft and Smooth, Rough and Bumpy: A Book About Touch

Think, Think, Think: Learning About Your Brain

Thump-Thump: Learning About Your Heart

Yum! A Book About Taste